30 MINUTES OR LESS | Sweet Treats

30 | Sweet

MINUTES OR LESS | Treats

p

This is a Parragon Book
First published in 2006

Parragon
Queen Street House
4 Queen Street
Bath BA1 1HE, UK

ISBN: 1-40547-385-1

Printed in China

Produced by the Bridgewater Book Company Ltd

Front cover photography by Laurie Evans
Front cover home economy by Carol Tennant

Notes for the Reader

This book uses metric and imperial measurements. Follow the same units of measurement throughout; do not mix metric and imperial. All spoon measurements are level: teaspoons are assumed to be 5 ml, and tablespoons are assumed to be 15 ml. Unless otherwise stated, milk is assumed to be full fat, eggs and individual vegetables are medium and pepper is freshly ground black pepper.

Recipes using raw or very lightly cooked eggs should be avoided by children, the elderly, pregnant women, convalescents and anyone suffering from an illness. Pregnant women and breast-feeding women are advised to avoid eating peanuts and peanut products.

Contents

Introduction 6

Chapter One
Chocolate 8

Chapter Two
Summer 28

Chapter Three
Winter 50

Chapter Four
Something Special 74

Index 96

Introduction

Aimed at the newcomer and experienced cook alike, this is an inspiring collection of quick and irresistible sweet treats. These fail-safe recipes guarantee rewarding results to satisfy a sweet tooth or round off a meal.

QUICKER, HEALTHIER AND MORE DELICIOUS

Bursting with delectable ideas, these recipes use easy-to-find, simple, fresh ingredients, and can be prepared in 30 minutes or less, enabling you to make delicious and beautifully presented food without an afternoon of cooking. Clear step-by-step instructions and full-colour photographs bring successful desserts and sweet treats within the realm of even the most inexperienced cook, and prove that it's possible to save time in the kitchen without compromising on flavour or quality. Several of the recipes will need a microwave for cooking, but most of the recipes can be completed using a stove or conventional oven.

The book is divided into four chapters: Chocolate, Summer, Winter and Something Special. Most people crave chocolate at some point, and here you will find a range of recipes, from luxurious desserts to tasty snacks, to cater for every whim and occasion. Make the most of summertime and enjoy the season's luscious berries as well as more exotic sun-ripened fruits in a variety of laid-back and chilled-out dishes. Winter, on the other hand, provides the perfect opportunity to focus on warming and comforting puddings, pancakes and deep-fried fruity fritters for a real end-of-meal treat. And Something Special offers some truly sumptuous yet sublimely easy suggestions for rounding off your dinner party in style.

You will recognize many old favourites in this book, from Chocolate Banana Sundae and Quick Tiramisù to Syllabub and Tropical Fruit Fool, but many of the recipes have been given a contemporary twist, being lighter in saturated fats and sugars to reflect the current move towards eating lesser amounts of these foods. The focus in the recipes is always on using the best-quality produce and if you use seasonally fresh ingredients, you're already well on the way to making a great-tasting dish. By investing in better-quality ingredients, you will need to do less to them and you can simply let their superior flavours speak for themselves.

Most people love sweet food, but there is no doubt that eating large quantities of puddings or cakes doesn't do much for your teeth or your figure. However, there is also no doubt that making and eating puddings can really lift your mood, and you should never feel that sweet food is something that must always be denied. Making puddings or sweet treats is one of those areas of cookery that can be truly magical – results can be rich and luxurious, as in Chocolate Zabaglione; warm and reassuring, as in Quick Syrup Sponge; or light and refreshing, as in Meringue with Lime Cream and Raspberries.

CHOOSING A PUDDING

The last course of a meal can be as simple or as complex as the rest of the meal, but it's important to remember that the last course sets the seal on the meal and should never be a disappointment. A pudding should echo the season, the weather and the mood of the occasion, and you do have to balance puddings with the rest of the meal. A rich, chocolatey pud after a heavy main course is a definite mistake, but a sharp Lemon Posset or a Mixed Fruit Salad might be just the thing. After a delicate fish dish, try something more subtle such as Chocolate Pancakes with Berry Compôte or something special like Warm Fruit Nests. For spicy foods, follow with Thai Bananas or Mini Coconut Pancakes.

EVEN QUICKER DESSERT IDEAS

For a last-minute supper with friends, some ice cream with a home-made sauce would be perfect. You can add your own touches to shop-bought ice-cream as well - simply remove from the freezer to soften, then stir in some chopped fruit, crushed biscuits, nuts or liqueur. Try whipping up mascarpone cheese or cream with lime and a little sugar to sweeten it and serve with a few fresh seasonal fruits. And although desserts needn't be elaborate creations, remember that just a swift sprinkling of nuts, grated chocolate or a dusting of sieved icing sugar or cocoa powder can transform an ordinary-looking dish into something extra special.

Chapter One
Chocolate

Mocha Fondue
10 minutes to the table

SERVES 4

ingredients

250 g/9 oz plain chocolate
   (at least 50% cocoa solids),
   broken into small pieces
100 ml/3 ½ fl oz double cream
1 tbsp instant coffee granules
3 tbsp coffee-flavoured liqueur,
   such as Kahlúa

DIPPERS
small sweet biscuits, such as amaretti
plain or coffee-flavoured marbled
   cake or sponge cake, cut into
   bite-sized pieces
whole seedless grapes
stoned and sliced firm peaches
   or nectarines

method

Arrange the dippers decoratively on a serving platter or individual serving plates and set aside.

Put the chocolate in the top of a double boiler or in a heatproof bowl set over a saucepan of barely simmering water. Add the cream and coffee granules and heat, stirring, until melted and smooth. Remove from the heat and stir in the liqueur, then carefully pour the mixture into a warmed fondue pot.

Using protective gloves, transfer the fondue pot to a lit tabletop burner. To serve, allow your guests to spear the dippers onto fondue forks and dip them into the fondue.

Chocolate Almond Balls
20 minutes to the table

MAKES 20

ingredients

150 g/5 ½ oz finely grated plain
    chocolate
55 g/2 oz finely chopped almonds
115 g/4 oz icing sugar
3 tbsp single cream

method

Put 115 g/4 oz of the chocolate in a bowl and spread the remaining chocolate evenly onto a plate.

Add the almonds to the chocolate in the bowl, then sift in the sugar. Stir together and add enough of the cream to form a firm mixture.

Take 1 heaped teaspoonful of the mixture at a time and roll into a ball. Continue until you have used up all the mixture. Drop each ball onto the plate of grated chocolate.

Roll the balls in the grated chocolate on the plate to coat thoroughly. To serve, put each ball in a paper sweet case.

variation

Other nuts, such as hazelnuts or macadamia nuts, could be used instead of the almonds.

Chocolate Zabaglione
15 minutes to the table

method

Put the egg yolks and sugar in a large heatproof bowl and whisk
together using a hand-held electric whisk until very pale.

Fold the chocolate into the egg mixture.

Gradually fold the Marsala into the chocolate mixture.

Set the bowl over a saucepan of gently simmering water and set the
electric whisk on the lowest speed or use a balloon whisk. Cook gently,
whisking constantly, until the mixture thickens; take care not to
overcook or the mixture will curdle.

Spoon the hot mixture into warmed individual glass dishes or coffee
cups and dust with cocoa powder. Serve the zabaglione as soon
as possible so that it is warm, light and fluffy, with amaretti biscuits, if
you like.

caution

Recipes using very lightly cooked eggs should be avoided by infants,
the elderly, pregnant women, convalescents and anyone suffering from
an illness.

cook's tip

Make the dessert just before serving because it will separate
if you let it stand. If it starts to curdle, remove from the heat
immediately and stand in a bowl of cold water to prevent further
cooking. Whisk vigorously until the mixture comes together again.

SERVES 4

ingredients

4 egg yolks

4 tbsp caster sugar

50 g/1 ¾ oz finely grated plain
   chocolate

125 ml/4 fl oz Marsala

cocoa powder, for dusting

amaretti biscuits, to serve (optional)

Chocolate Pancakes with Berry Compôte

30 minutes to the table

SERVES 8-10

ingredients

115 g/4 oz plain flour
25 g/1 oz cocoa powder
pinch of salt
1 egg
25 g/1 oz caster sugar
350 ml/12 fl oz milk
50 g/1¾ oz butter
icing sugar, for dusting
pouring cream, to serve

BERRY COMPÔTE

150 g/5½ oz fresh blackberries
150 g/5½ oz fresh blueberries
225 g/8 oz fresh raspberries
55 g/2 oz caster sugar
juice of ½ lemon
½ tsp ground mixed spice (optional)

method

Preheat the oven to 140ºC/275ºF/Gas Mark 1. Sift the flour, cocoa powder and salt together into a large bowl. Make a well in the centre. Beat the egg, caster sugar and half the milk together in a separate bowl. Pour into the well. Beat the dry ingredients into the liquid, gradually drawing them in from the side, until a smooth batter is formed. Gradually beat in the remaining milk. Pour into a jug.

Heat an 18-cm/7-inch non-stick frying pan over a medium heat and add 1 teaspoon of the butter. When the butter has melted, pour in enough batter just to cover the base, then swirl around the frying pan while tilting it to make an even layer. Cook for 30 seconds and then lift up the edge of the pancake to check if it is cooked. Loosen around the edge, then flip over with a spatula. Cook until the base is golden brown.

Transfer the pancake to a warmed plate and keep warm in the preheated oven while you cook the remaining batter, adding the remaining butter to the frying pan as necessary. Make a stack of the pancakes with baking paper in between each pancake.

To make the compôte, put the berries, caster sugar, lemon juice and mixed spice, if using, in a saucepan over a low heat. Cook, stirring gently, until the sugar has dissolved and the berries are warmed through. Put the pancakes on warmed serving plates and spoon the compôte over. Fold the pancake and dust with icing sugar. Serve with pouring cream.

Chocolate Squares
30 minutes to the table

MAKES AROUND 50

ingredients

115 g/4 oz butter, plus extra for
   greasing
55 g/2 oz caster sugar
115 g/4 oz cocoa powder
115 g/4 oz drinking chocolate powder

method

Grease an 18-cm/7-inch square shallow cake tin or a 20-x 15-cm/
8- x 6-inch shallow baking tin. Melt the butter in a saucepan over a low
heat. Remove from the heat and stir in the sugar.

   Sift the cocoa powder and drinking chocolate powder into the butter
mixture, then beat vigorously together until smooth.

   Turn the mixture into the prepared tin, cover and chill in the
refrigerator until set. When the chocolate has set, cut into 2.5-cm/
1-inch squares using a sharp knife.

Chocolate Banana Sundae

15 minutes to the table

method

To make the chocolate sauce, put the chocolate in a heatproof bowl with the syrup and butter set over a saucepan of barely simmering water. Heat, stirring, until melted and smooth. Remove the bowl from the heat and stir in the brandy, if using.

Whip the cream in a separate bowl until it is just holding its shape. Peel and slice the bananas. Put a scoop of ice cream in the bottom of 4 tall sundae dishes. Top with slices of banana, some chocolate sauce, a spoonful of the whipped cream and a generous sprinkling of nuts.

Repeat the layers, finishing with a good dollop of the whipped cream, sprinkled with nuts and a little grated or flaked chocolate. Serve with fan wafers.

variation

For a traditional banana split, halve the bananas lengthways and put on a plate with 2 scoops of ice cream between. Top with the cream and sprinkle with the nuts. Serve with the Glossy Chocolate Sauce poured over the top.

SERVES 4

ingredients

GLOSSY CHOCOLATE SAUCE

55 g/2 oz plain chocolate, broken into
   small pieces

4 tbsp golden syrup

1 tbsp butter

1 tbsp brandy or dark rum (optional)

SUNDAE

150 ml/5 fl oz double cream

4 bananas

8-12 scoops good quality vanilla
   ice cream

75 g/2 ¾ oz flaked or chopped
   almonds, toasted

grated or flaked chocolate,
   for sprinkling

4 fan wafers, to serve

Snowy Chocolate Crispies

25 minutes to the table

MAKES 24

ingredients

225 g/8 oz butter

200 g/7 oz golden syrup

225 g/8 oz plain chocolate, broken
   into small pieces

200 g/7 oz puffed rice cereal

225 g/8 oz white chocolate, broken
   into small pieces

chopped hazelnuts or almonds,
   to decorate

method

Melt the butter and syrup in a small saucepan over a low heat. Add the plain chocolate and heat, stirring, until melted and smooth.

Remove from the heat and add the puffed rice. Stir thoroughly to ensure that the rice is evenly coated. Spoon the mixture into 24 paper fairy cake cases and leave to set for 5 minutes.

Meanwhile, put the white chocolate in a heatproof bowl set over a saucepan of barely simmering water and heat until melted. Pour a teaspoonful of the melted white chocolate on top of each cake, sprinkle with chopped nuts to decorate and leave to set for at least 5 minutes before serving.

Mocha Coconut Clusters

30 minutes to the table

method

Line 2–3 baking sheets with baking paper. Put the chocolate and butter in a heatproof bowl set over a saucepan of barely simmering water and heat, stirring, until melted and smooth. Remove the bowl from the heat.

Stir the coffee granules into the chocolate until dissolved, then stir in the coconut.

Put heaped teaspoonfuls of the mixture on the prepared baking sheets, cover and chill in the refrigerator until set. To serve, put each cluster in a paper sweet case.

cook's tip

If you wish, toast the coconut before you add it to the mixture, to bring out its full flavour. To do this, put in a large dry frying pan over a low heat and cook, stirring constantly, until golden brown.

MAKES 30

ingredients

115 g/4 oz milk chocolate, broken
    into small pieces
2 tbsp butter
1 tsp instant coffee granules
55 g/2 oz desiccated coconut

Chocolate Popcorn
30 minutes to the table

method

Preheat the oven to 150°C/300°F/Gas Mark 2. Heat the oil in a large, heavy-based saucepan over a high heat. Add the popcorn, cover and cook, shaking the saucepan vigorously and frequently, for 2 minutes, or until the popping stops. Turn into a large bowl.

Heat the butter, sugar, syrup and milk in a saucepan over a low heat, stirring, until the butter and syrup have melted. Bring to the boil, without stirring, and boil for 2 minutes. Remove from the heat, add the chocolate chips and stir until melted and smooth.

Pour the chocolate mixture over the popcorn and toss together until evenly coated. Spread the mixture onto a large baking sheet.

Bake the popcorn in the preheated oven for 15 minutes, or until crisp. Leave to cool before serving.

MAKES ABOUT 250 G/9 OZ

ingredients

3 tbsp sunflower oil
70 g/2 ½ oz popcorn
25 g/1 oz butter
55 g/2 oz soft light brown sugar
2 tbsp golden syrup
1 tbsp milk
55 g/2 oz plain chocolate chips

Chapter Two
Summer

Lemon Posset
15 minutes to the table

SERVES 4

ingredients

grated rind and juice of 1 large lemon
4 tbsp dry white wine
55 g/2 oz caster sugar
300 ml/10 fl oz double cream
2 egg whites
lemon slices, to decorate
langues de chat biscuits, to serve

method

Mix the lemon rind and juice, wine and sugar together in a bowl. Stir until the sugar has dissolved. Add the cream and beat with a hand-held electric whisk until soft peaks form.

Whisk the egg whites in a separate, spotlessly clean, grease-free bowl until stiff, then gently fold into the cream mixture.

Spoon the mixture into tall glasses, cover and leave to chill in the refrigerator until required. Serve decorated with lemon slices and accompanied by langues de chat biscuits.

caution

Use only the very freshest of eggs for this dish. Recipes using raw eggs should be avoided by infants, the elderly, pregnant women, convalescents and anyone suffering from an illness.

variation

Replace the lemon with the grated rind and juice of 1 orange, decorate with orange slices and serve with amaretti biscuits.

Figs with Orange Blossom

20 minutes to the table

method

To toast the almonds for the decoration, if using, put in a dry frying pan over a medium heat and cook, stirring constantly, until lightly browned. Take care that the almonds do not burn. Immediately tip out of the frying pan and set aside.

To make the orange-blossom cream, put the crème fraîche in a small bowl and stir in the orange-flower water, honey and orange rind. Taste and add a little extra orange-flower water if necessary, and sweeten with a little more honey, if you like.

To serve, cut the stems off the figs, but do not peel them. Stand the figs upright with the pointed end upwards. Cut each fig into quarters, without cutting all the way through, so that you can open them out into attractive 'flowers'.

If you are using fig leaves to decorate, put 1 in the centre of each serving plate. Arrange 2 figs on top of each leaf and spoon a small amount of the orange-blossom cream alongside them. Sprinkle the cream with the toasted flaked almonds, if you like, just before serving.

SERVES 4

ingredients

8 fresh large figs

ORANGE-BLOSSOM CREAM
115 g/4 oz crème fraîche
4 tbsp orange-flower water, or
    to taste
1 tsp clear orange-blossom honey, or
    to taste
finely grated rind of ½ orange

TO DECORATE
2 tbsp flaked almonds, toasted
    (optional)
4 fresh large fig leaves,
    rinsed and dried (optional)

Summer Fruit Nectarines

25 minutes to the table

method

Preheat the barbecue. Cut 8 x 18-cm/7-inch squares of foil. Wash the nectarines and pat dry with kitchen paper. Halve and remove and discard the stones. Put each nectarine half, stone cavity side up, on a square of foil.

Fill each nectarine half with fruit, then top each one with about 1 teaspoon lemon juice, then 1 teaspoon honey.

Close the foil around each nectarine half to make a parcel, then cook over hot coals for 10-15 minutes according to your taste.

Transfer the nectarines to serving plates and serve immediately with crème fraîche, mascarpone cheese or ice cream.

SERVES 4

ingredients

4 large nectarines

115 g/4 oz mixed summer fruit, such as blackberries, blueberries and raspberries, thawed if frozen

3 tbsp lemon juice

3 tbsp clear honey

crème fraîche, mascarpone cheese or ice cream, to serve

Caribbean Pineapple
20 minutes to the table

SERVES 6

ingredients

2 tbsp raisins

4 tbsp rum

175 g/6 oz good quality
   plain chocolate

1 pineapple

4 tbsp unsalted butter

6 tbsp golden syrup

fresh mint sprigs, to decorate

method

Put the raisins in a heatproof bowl and pour over the rum. Set aside to soak and plump up. Break up the chocolate into fairly small pieces.

Meanwhile, preheat the grill to medium. Cut off the leafy top and the base of the pineapple and discard. Stand the pineapple upright and slice off the skin. Remove any remaining 'eyes' with the tip of a small, sharp knife. Cut the pineapple in half lengthways and cut out the hard, woody core, then slice the flesh.

Arrange the pineapple slices on a baking sheet in a single layer and dot with half the butter. Cook under the preheated grill, turning frequently, for 5-6 minutes until just beginning to brown.

Meanwhile, to make the sauce, add the syrup and the remaining butter to the raisins and set the bowl over a saucepan of barely simmering water. Heat, stirring, until the syrup and butter have melted, then add the chocolate and heat, stirring, until melted and smooth.

Divide the pineapple between warmed serving plates, spoon over the chocolate sauce, decorate with mint sprigs and serve immediately.

variation

This would also work well with other fruit, such as halved nectarines, wedges of fresh mango or peeled bananas halved lengthways.

Thai Bananas
15 minutes to the table

SERVES 6

ingredients

350 ml/12 fl oz canned coconut milk

2 tbsp granulated sugar

½ tsp salt

6 slightly under-ripe bananas, peeled
   and cut into 5-cm/2-inch lengths

1 tbsp toasted sesame seeds,
   to decorate

method

Put the coconut milk, sugar and salt in a saucepan over a low heat and stir until the sugar has dissolved. Add the banana pieces and cook, stirring occasionally, for 5 minutes, or until the bananas are soft but not mushy.

Divide the mixture between 6 small bowls. Scatter the sesame seeds over to decorate and serve immediately.

Chargrilled Fruit
30 minutes to the table

method

Preheat the grill to medium. Cut off the leafy top and the base of the pineapple and discard. Stand the pineapple upright and slice off the skin. Remove any remaining 'eyes' with the tip of a small, sharp knife. Slice the flesh into rings and cut out the hard, woody core. Set 4 rings aside and cover and store the remainder in the refrigerator for another day.

Halve the pawpaw and scoop out the seeds with a metal spoon and discard. Peel and slice the flesh. Set aside 4 slices and cover and store the remainder in the refrigerator for another day.

Slice the mango in half through to the stone, then twist the halves to remove the flesh from the stone. Peel and slice the flesh, set 4 slices aside and cover and store the remainder in the refrigerator for another day.

Mix the honey, orange and lemon rind and ginger together in a bowl. Arrange the pineapple, pawpaw and mango on the grill rack with the kiwi fruit, nectarines and bananas. Brush the honey glaze over the fruit.

Cook the fruit under the preheated grill for 10 minutes, brushing with the glaze and turning frequently. Divide between 4 serving plates and serve immediately.

cook's tip

Use a single-flower honey, if possible. Try clover, acacia, orange blossom or lavender – they will impart a delicious flavour to the chargrilled fruit.

SERVES 4

ingredients

1 pineapple

1 pawpaw

1 mango

6 tbsp clear honey

grated rind of 1 orange

grated rind of 1 lemon

2.5-cm/1-inch piece fresh
    root ginger, grated

4 kiwi fruit, peeled and sliced

2 nectarines, peeled, halved
    and stoned

2 bananas, peeled and halved

Tropical Fruit Fool
30 minutes to the table

SERVES 4

ingredients

1 mango

2 kiwi fruit

1 banana

2 tbsp lime juice

½ tsp finely grated lime rind, plus
   extra finely pared thin strips of zest
   to decorate

2 egg whites

425 ml/15 fl oz canned low-fat
   custard

½ tsp vanilla extract

2 passion fruit

method

Slice the mango in half through to the stone, then twist the halves
to remove the flesh from the stone. Peel and roughly chop the flesh.
Put in a food processor or blender and process until smooth.
Alternatively, mash with a fork in a bowl.

   Peel the kiwi fruit, chop the flesh into small pieces and put in a bowl.
Peel and chop the banana and add to the bowl. Add the lime juice and
grated rind and toss to coat well.

   Whisk the egg whites in a separate, spotlessly clean, grease-free bowl
until stiff, then gently fold in the custard and vanilla extract until
thoroughly mixed.

   Alternately layer the chopped fruit, mango purée and custard
mixture in 4 tall glasses, finishing with the custard on top. Cover and
chill in the refrigerator for 15 minutes.

   Meanwhile, halve the passion fruit and scoop out the seeds and
discard. To serve, spoon the passion fruit pulp over the fruit fools and
decorate each serving with thin strips of lime zest.

caution

Use only the very freshest of eggs for this dish. Recipes using raw eggs
should be avoided by infants, the elderly, pregnant women,
convalescents and anyone suffering from an illness.

Ice Cream Sauces
30 minutes to the table

method

To make the port sauce, blend 4 tablespoons of the port with the cornflour in a small bowl to make a smooth paste. Pour the remainder of the port into a saucepan and bring to the boil. Stir in the cornflour paste and cook, stirring constantly, for 1 minute, or until thickened. Remove from the heat and leave to cool. Pour into a bowl, cover and chill in the refrigerator until required.

Meanwhile, to make the chocolate sauce, put the cream, butter and sugar in a heatproof bowl set over a saucepan of barely simmering water and heat, stirring constantly, until the butter has melted and the sugar has dissolved. Remove the bowl from the heat and leave to cool slightly. Add the chocolate and stir until melted and smooth. Stir in the rum, if using, then leave to cool to room temperature before serving.

To make the berry sauce, put all the ingredients in a small, heavy-based saucepan over a low heat and heat, stirring gently, until the fruit juices run and the sugar has dissolved. Purée with a hand-held blender or in a food processor. Push through a nylon sieve into a serving bowl to remove the seeds. Add more sugar, if necessary. Serve warm or cold.

Serve scoops of ice cream with a little of the 3 sauces on the side. Serve the remaining sauce in jugs or bowls.

SERVES 6

ingredients
vanilla or chocolate ice cream,
   to serve

PORT SAUCE
350 ml/12 fl oz ruby port
2 tsp cornflour

CHOCOLATE SAUCE
150 ml/5 fl oz double cream
4 tbsp unsalted butter
55 g/2 oz soft light brown sugar
175 g/6 oz plain chocolate, broken
   into small pieces
2 tbsp dark rum (optional)

BERRY SAUCE
225 g/8 oz fresh berries, such as
   blackberries or raspberries
2 tbsp water
2–3 tbsp caster sugar, to taste
2 tbsp fruit liqueur, such as crème de
   cassis or crème de framboise

Mixed Fruit Salad
20 minutes to the table

SERVES 4

ingredients

1 pawpaw
1 small pineapple
1 small melon
2 oranges
12 lychees
2 bananas
grated rind and juice of 1 lime, plus
   extra finely pared thin strips of zest
   to decorate
2 tbsp caster sugar

method

Halve the pawpaw and scoop out the seeds with a metal spoon and discard. Peel the halves.

Cut off the leafy top and the base of the pineapple and discard. Stand the pineapple upright and slice off the skin. Remove any remaining 'eyes' with the tip of a small, sharp knife. Slice the flesh into rings and cut out the hard, woody core.

Halve the melon and scoop out the seeds with a metal spoon and discard. Peel the halves and cut into thin wedges.

Cut off the rind and white pith from the oranges. Cut the orange slices out from between the membranes.

Peel the lychees, then peel and thickly slice the bananas.

Arrange all the prepared fruit on a serving platter. Scatter the thin strips of lime zest over the fruit salad to decorate.

Mix the grated lime rind and juice and sugar together in a bowl. Pour over the salad and serve.

Warm Fruit Compôte
10 minutes to the table

SERVES 4

ingredients

4 fresh plums, halved and stoned

225 g/8 oz fresh raspberries

225 g/8 oz fresh strawberries, hulled
  and halved

2 tbsp light muscovado sugar

2 tbsp dry white wine

2 star anise

1 cinnamon stick

4 cloves

method

Put all the ingredients in a large, heavy-based saucepan over a low heat and stir gently until the sugar has dissolved.

Cover tightly and simmer very gently for 5 minutes, or until the fruit is tender but still retains its shape. Do not allow the mixture to boil.

Remove and discard the star anise, cinnamon stick and cloves and serve the compôte warm.

Chapter Three
Winter

Baked Banana with Sin-free Chocolate Sauce

15 minutes to the table

SERVES 1

ingredients

1 small banana

2 tsp golden syrup

3 tsp cocoa powder

method

Preheat the oven to 180ºC/350ºF/Gas Mark 4.

Bake the banana in its skin in the preheated oven directly on the oven shelf for 10 minutes, or until the skin is black, turning halfway through the cooking time.

Meanwhile, heat the syrup in a small saucepan over a medium heat for 2–3 minutes or heat in a medium-low microwave oven for 1 minute, or until very runny. Add the cocoa powder and stir until smooth and chocolate-like. Keep warm.

Remove the banana from the oven and leave to cool slightly. When cool enough to handle, remove and discard the skin and transfer the banana to a serving plate. Pour over the warm chocolate sauce and serve immediately.

Toffee Apple Slices
25 minutes to the table

method

Preheat the oven to 140°C/275°F/Gas Mark 1. To make the batter, sift the flour into a large bowl. Make a well in the centre. Beat the egg and water together in a separate bowl. Pour into the well in the flour. Beat the flour into the liquid, gradually drawing it in from the side, until a smooth, thick batter is formed.

Heat enough oil for deep-frying in a preheated wok, deep-fat fryer or large heavy-based saucepan until it reaches 180–190°C/350–375°F, or until a cube of bread browns in 30 seconds. Spear each apple slice with a fork, 1 at a time, and dip in the batter to coat. Add to the oil, in batches, and cook for 1 minute on each side, or until golden and puffed up. Remove with a slotted spoon and drain on kitchen paper. Keep warm in the preheated oven while you cook the remaining apple slices.

To make the toffee syrup, heat the sesame oil in a small, heavy-based saucepan over a high heat. When beginning to smoke, add the sugar and cook, stirring constantly, until the mixture caramelizes and turns golden. Remove from the heat, stir in the sesame seeds and pour into a large, shallow baking tin.

Put the tin over a very low heat, add the apple slices and turn once in the syrup to coat. Dip the apple slices in a bowl of cold water, then serve immediately.

cook's tip

Work quickly to ensure that the syrup does not set and in order to seal the syrup on each apple slice.

SERVES 6

ingredients

vegetable or groundnut oil, for
   deep-frying
4 apples, peeled, cored and each cut
   lengthways into 8 slices

BATTER
115 g/4 oz plain flour
1 egg
125 ml/4 fl oz cold water

TOFFEE SYRUP
4 tbsp sesame oil
225 g/8 oz granulated sugar
2 tbsp sesame seeds, toasted

Flambé Peaches
15 minutes to the table

SERVES 4

ingredients

3 tbsp unsalted butter

3 tbsp muscovado sugar

4 tbsp orange juice

4 peaches, peeled, halved and stoned

2 tbsp almond liqueur or
   peach brandy

4 tbsp flaked almonds, toasted

method

Put the butter, sugar and orange juice in a large, heavy-based frying pan over a low heat and stir constantly until the butter has melted and the sugar has dissolved.

Add the peach halves and cook for 1-2 minutes on each side, or until golden.

Add the almond liqueur and ignite with a match or taper. When the flames have died down, transfer to serving dishes, sprinkle with the toasted flaked almonds and serve immediately.

Mexican Glazed Pumpkin

25 minutes to the table

method

Cut the pumpkin into wedges and scoop out the seeds with a metal spoon and discard. Arrange in a large, flameproof casserole.

Mix the sugar and mixed spice together in a bowl, then spoon into the spaces between the pumpkin wedges. Add the water, pouring it down the side of the casserole so that it doesn't wash away the sugar.

Cover and cook over a low heat for 20 minutes, or until the pumpkin is tender.

Transfer the pumpkin wedges to a serving dish and pour over the sugary glaze. Serve immediately.

cook's tip

Keep an eye on the water level while the pumpkin is cooking and top up with more hot water, if necessary.

SERVES 4

ingredients
900 g/2 lb pumpkin
425 g/15 oz light muscovado sugar
1 tsp ground mixed spice
225 ml/8 fl oz water

Pineapple Bake
20 minutes to the table

method

Preheat the oven to 240°C/475°F/Gas Mark 9. Cut off the leafy top and the base of the pineapple and discard. Stand the pineapple upright and slice off the skin. Remove any remaining 'eyes' with the tip of a small, sharp knife. Cut the pineapple in half lengthways and cut out the hard, woody core, then slice the flesh.

Arrange the pineapple slices in a large, ovenproof dish and sprinkle over the sultanas and raisins. Drizzle with half the maple syrup and half the rum. Bake in the preheated oven for 5 minutes.

Meanwhile, mix the remaining maple syrup and rum, egg yolk, cornflour, vanilla extract and ginger together in a bowl. Whisk the egg whites in a separate, spotlessly clean, grease-free bowl until soft peaks form. Stir 2 tablespoons of the egg whites into the egg yolk mixture, then fold the remaining egg yolk mixture into the egg whites.

Spread the topping over the hot pineapple, sift the sugar over the top and bake in the oven for a further 5 minutes, or until golden brown. Serve immediately.

cook's tip

There are two important points to note: make sure that you buy genuine maple syrup (not maple-flavoured syrup) and pure vanilla extract, which is made from crushed vanilla pods.

SERVES 6

ingredients

1 pineapple
4 tbsp sultanas
2 tbsp raisins
4 tbsp maple syrup
4 tbsp white rum, such as Bacardi
1 egg yolk
1 tbsp cornflour
½ tsp vanilla extract
¼ tsp ground ginger
2 egg whites
2 tbsp muscovado sugar

Apple Pancakes with Maple Syrup Butter

25 minutes to the table

SERVES 4-6

ingredients

200 g/7 oz self-raising flour

1 tsp ground cinnamon

100 g/3½ oz caster sugar

1 egg

200 ml/7 fl oz milk

2 apples, peeled, cored and grated

1 tsp butter

MAPLE SYRUP BUTTER

85 g/3 oz butter, softened

3 tbsp maple syrup

method

Preheat the oven to 140°C/275°F/Gas Mark 1. Sift the flour and cinnamon together into a large bowl. Stir in the sugar. Make a well in the centre of the dry ingredients. Beat the egg and milk together in a separate bowl. Pour into the well in the dry ingredients. Beat the dry ingredients into the liquid, gradually drawing them in from the side, until a smooth batter is formed, then stir in the apple.

Heat the butter in a large, non-stick frying pan over a medium heat until melted and bubbling. Add 3-4 tablespoons of the batter, spaced well apart. Cook for 1-2 minutes, or until beginning to bubble lightly on the top and looking set, then flip over with a spatula or palette knife. Cook on the other side for 30 seconds, or until cooked through and golden brown. Transfer the pancakes to a warmed plate and keep warm in the preheated oven while you cook the remaining batter (it is not necessary to add extra butter to the frying pan). Make a stack of the pancakes with baking paper in between each pancake.

To make the Maple Syrup Butter, melt the butter and syrup in a saucepan over a low heat, stirring until smooth and combined. To serve, put the pancakes on serving dishes and spoon over the maple syrup butter. Serve immediately.

Apple Fritters
20 minutes to the table

SERVES 4

ingredients

sunflower oil, for deep-frying

1 large egg

pinch of salt

175 ml/6 fl oz water

55 g/2 oz plain flour

2 tsp ground cinnamon

55 g/2 oz caster sugar

4 eating apples, peeled and cored

method

Preheat the oven to 140°C/275°F/Gas Mark 1. Heat the oil in a preheated wok, deep-fat fryer or large, heavy-based saucepan until it reaches 180–190°C/350–375°F, or until a cube of bread browns in 30 seconds.

Put the egg and salt in a bowl and whisk together using a hand-held electric whisk until frothy. Quickly whisk in the water and flour. Do not overbeat the batter – it need not be completely smooth.

Mix the cinnamon and sugar together in a shallow dish and set aside.

Slice the apples into 5-mm/¼-inch thick rings. Spear with a fork, 1 slice at a time, and dip in the batter to coat. Add to the hot oil, in batches, and cook for 1 minute on each side, or until golden and puffed up. Remove with a slotted spoon and drain on kitchen paper. Keep warm in the preheated oven while you cook the remaining fritters.

Transfer to a large serving plate, sprinkle with the cinnamon sugar and serve immediately.

cook's tip

The best and easiest way to core an apple is to use an apple corer. Push the corer into the stalk end of the apple and twist to cut around the core, then pull it out and discard.

variations

Replace the apple with 1 small pineapple, peeled, sliced into rings and cored, or use 4 bananas, peeled and sliced.

Mini Coconut Pancakes
20 minutes to the table

method

Preheat the oven to 140°C/275°F/Gas Mark 1. Put the creamed coconut in a heatproof bowl, pour in the water and stir until dissolved.

Sift the flour into a separate large bowl and stir in the sugar. Make a well in the centre. Beat the eggs and half the milk together in another bowl. Pour into the well in the dry ingredients. Beat the dry ingredients into the liquid, gradually drawing them in from the side, until a smooth, thick batter is formed. Gradually beat in the remaining milk and then the coconut mixture. Stir in the desiccated coconut.

Melt a little of the butter in a large, heavy-based frying pan. Add 3–4 tablespoons of the batter, spaced well apart. Cook the batter for 1–2 minutes, or until it begins to bubble lightly on top and looks set, then flip over with a spatula or palette knife. Cook on the other side for 30 seconds, or until cooked through and golden brown. Transfer the pancakes to a warmed plate and keep warm in the preheated oven while you cook the remaining batter, adding the remaining butter to the frying pan as necessary. Make a stack of the pancakes with baking paper in between each pancake.

Serve the pancakes warm with the melon slices.

SERVES 4

ingredients

55 g/2 oz creamed coconut, chopped
150 ml/5 fl oz boiling water
225 g/8 oz plain flour
2 tbsp caster sugar
2 eggs
450 ml/16 fl oz milk
25 g/1 oz desiccated coconut
55 g/2 oz butter
½ melon, halved, deseeded, peeled
    and thinly sliced, to serve

Poached Mixed Spice Pears

20 minutes to the table

SERVES 4

ingredients

4 fresh large pears
300 ml/10 fl oz orange juice
2 tsp ground mixed spice
75 g/2¾ oz raisins
2 tbsp soft light brown sugar
strips of orange rind, to decorate

method

Core the pears with an apple corer. Using a sharp knife, peel and halve the pears.

Put the pear halves in a large saucepan. Add the orange juice, mixed spice, raisins and sugar and heat over a low heat, stirring, until the sugar has dissolved. Bring the mixture to the boil and boil for 1 minute.

Reduce the heat to low and simmer for 10 minutes, or until the pears are cooked but still fairly firm – test by inserting the tip of a sharp knife into the fruit.

Remove the pears with a slotted spoon and transfer to individual serving plates. Decorate with strips of orange rind and serve hot with the syrup from the saucepan.

cook's tip

This dessert is refreshing at the end of a big meal. It can also be served cold.

Churros
25 minutes to the table

SERVES 4

ingredients

225 ml/8 fl oz water
grated rind of 1 lemon
85 g/3 oz butter
⅛ tsp salt
140 g/5 oz plain flour
¼ tsp ground cinnamon,
    plus extra for dusting
½–1 tsp vanilla extract
3 eggs
olive oil, for frying
caster sugar, for sprinkling

method

Put the water and lemon rind in a heavy-based saucepan over a medium heat. Bring to the boil, add the butter and salt and cook for a few seconds until the butter has melted.

Add the flour, all at once, cinnamon and vanilla extract, then remove from the heat and stir vigorously until the mixture forms the consistency of mashed potatoes.

Beat in the eggs, 1 at a time, using a wooden spoon; if you have difficulty incorporating the eggs to a smooth mixture, use a potato masher, then when it is mixed, return to a wooden spoon and mix until smooth.

Heat 2.5 cm/1 inch of oil in a deep frying pan until it reaches 180–190°C/350–375°F, or until a cube of bread browns in 30 seconds.

Put the batter in a piping bag fitted with a wide star nozzle. Pipe 13-cm/5-inch lengths directly into the hot oil, in 2–3 batches, spaced 7.5–10 cm/3–4 inches apart. Cook for 2 minutes on each side, or until golden brown. Remove with a slotted spoon and drain on kitchen paper.

Sprinkle generously with sugar and dust with cinnamon to taste. Serve either hot or at room temperature.

Sponge Cake with Custard

20 minutes to the table

method

Grease a 1.5-litre/2¾-pint pudding basin with a little of the butter. Spoon the syrup into the prepared basin.

Beat the remaining butter with the sugar in a bowl until pale and fluffy. Gradually add the eggs, beating well after each addition.

Sift the flour and baking powder together, then gently fold into the butter mixture using a large metal spoon. Add enough water to give a soft, dropping consistency. Spoon the mixture into the basin and level the surface.

Cover with microwave-safe film, leaving a small space to let the air escape. Cook in a microwave oven on high for 4 minutes, then remove and leave the pudding to stand for 5 minutes while it continues to cook.

Turn the pudding out onto a serving plate. Serve with custard.

SERVES 4

ingredients

125 g/4½ oz butter or margarine

4 tbsp golden syrup

85 g/3 oz caster sugar

2 eggs, lightly beaten

125 g/4½ oz self-raising flour

1 tsp baking powder

about 2 tbsp warm water

custard, to serve

Chapter Four

Something Special

Syllabub
15 minutes to the table

SERVES 6

ingredients

175 ml/6 fl oz Madeira
2 tbsp brandy
grated rind of 1 lemon
125 ml/4 fl oz lemon juice
115 g/4 oz caster sugar
600 ml/1 pint double cream
10 amaretti or ratafia biscuits,
    crumbled
ground cinnamon, to serve
lemon slices, to decorate

method

Mix the Madeira, brandy, lemon rind and juice and sugar together in a bowl until well combined.

Add the cream and beat with a hand-held electric whisk until the mixture is thick.

Divide the crumbled biscuits between 6 long-stemmed glasses or sundae dishes. On top of this, fill each glass or dish with the syllabub mixture, cover and chill in the refrigerator until required.

To serve, dust the surface of each dessert with a little ground cinnamon and decorate with lemon slices.

cook's tip

Madeira is a fortified wine from the island of the same name. It may be dry, medium or sweet. Sweet Madeira is best for this recipe.

Quick Tiramisù
15 minutes to the table

method

Put the mascarpone cheese, egg yolk and yogurt in a large bowl and beat together until smooth.

Whisk the egg white in a separate, spotlessly clean, grease-free bowl until stiff but not dry, then whisk in the sugar and gently fold into the cheese mixture. Divide half the mixture between 4 sundae glasses.

Mix the rum and coffee together in a shallow dish. Dip the sponge fingers into the rum mixture, break them in half, or into smaller pieces if necessary, and divide between the glasses.

Stir any remaining coffee mixture into the remaining cheese mixture and divide between the glasses.

Sprinkle with the grated chocolate. Serve immediately or cover and chill in the refrigerator until required.

caution

Use only the very freshest of eggs for this dish. Recipes using raw eggs should be avoided by infants, the elderly, pregnant women, convalescents and anyone suffering from an illness.

cook's tip

Mascarpone is an Italian soft cream cheese made from cow's milk. It has a rich, silky smooth texture and a deliciously creamy flavour. It can be eaten as it is with fresh fruit or flavoured with coffee or chocolate.

SERVES 4

ingredients

225 g/8 oz mascarpone cheese or
full-fat soft cheese
1 egg, separated
2 tbsp natural yogurt
2 tbsp caster sugar
2 tbsp dark rum
2 tbsp cold strong black coffee
8 sponge fingers
2 tbsp grated plain chocolate

Danish Layered Cake
20 minutes to the table

SERVES 6

ingredients

225 g/8 oz rye bread, crusts removed
2 tbsp caster sugar
25 g/1 oz unsalted butter
900 g/2 lb apple purée or apple sauce
225 g/8 oz blackcurrant jam
300 ml/10 fl oz double cream

method

Tear the bread into pieces, put in a food processor and process until crumbs form. Transfer to a bowl and stir in the sugar.

Melt the butter in a large, heavy-based frying pan over a medium heat. Add the breadcrumb mixture and cook, stirring frequently, for 3-5 minutes, or until crisp. Remove from the heat and leave to cool slightly.

Spoon half the apple purée into the base of a glass serving dish. Cover the purée with half the jam, then spoon over half the breadcrumb mixture. Repeat these layers, ending with a final layer of breadcrumb mixture.

Put the cream in a bowl and beat with a hand-held electric whisk until stiff, then spread over the top of the dessert. Serve immediately or cover and chill in the refrigerator until required.

cook's tip

The contrasts in this dessert derive from using rye bread, which has a distinctive flavour and texture, for the crumbs. You could use German black bread instead, made from a mixture of rye and cornmeal.

Banana Soufflés

20 minutes to the table

SERVES 4

ingredients

sunflower or corn oil, for brushing

2 bananas

1 tbsp lemon or lime juice

1 tbsp Malibu or coconut liqueur

4 eggs, separated

55 g/2 oz caster sugar

icing sugar, for dusting (optional)

method

Preheat the oven to 230°C/450°F/Gas Mark 8. Lightly brush 4 x 350-ml/12-fl oz soufflé dishes with oil. Peel the bananas and cut into 2.5-cm/1-inch lengths. Put the bananas, lemon juice and Malibu in a food processor or blender and process to a smooth purée. Add the egg yolks and 1 teaspoon of the caster sugar and process briefly again to mix. Scrape into a bowl.

Whisk the egg whites in a separate, spotlessly clean, grease-free bowl until stiff, then whisk in the remaining caster sugar, 1 tablespoon at a time, until stiff and glossy. Fold 1 tablespoon of the egg whites into the banana mixture, then gently fold in the remainder.

Spoon the soufflé mixture into the prepared dishes and make a rim with the end of a teaspoon. Put on a baking sheet and bake in the preheated oven for 8 minutes, or until well risen and golden. Dust with icing sugar, if you like, and serve immediately.

caution

Recipes using lightly cooked eggs should be avoided by infants, the elderly, pregnant women, convalescents and anyone suffering from an illness.

cook's tip

To whisk egg whites successfully, make sure that they are as fresh as possible and at room temperature. Adding a pinch of cream of tartar can help them to achieve their maximum volume and stiffness.

Meringue with Lime Cream and Raspberries

10 minutes to the table

method

Mix the yogurt, sugar and grated lime rind and juice together in a bowl until well blended.

   Put the meringue nest on a serving plate. Pour in the yogurt mixture and sprinkle with the raspberries. Decorate with thin strips of lime zest and serve immediately.

cook's tip

You can substitute thawed frozen fruits of the forest for the raspberries or use other fresh fruit in season.

SERVES 1

ingredients

2½ tbsp natural bio-yogurt

2 tsp icing sugar

grated rind and juice of ¼ lime, plus
    extra finely pared thin strips of
    zest to decorate

1 meringue nest

25 g/1 oz fresh raspberries

Sweet Potato Dessert
25 minutes to the table

SERVES 4

ingredients

1 kg/2 lb 4 oz sweet potatoes
850 ml/1½ pints milk
175 g/6 oz sugar
chopped almonds, to decorate

method

Using a sharp knife, peel the sweet potatoes. Rinse, then slice. Put in a large saucepan, pour over 600 ml/1 pint of the milk and cook over a low heat for 15 minutes, or until soft enough to be mashed.

Remove from the heat and mash thoroughly until completely smooth. Add the sugar and the remaining milk and stir gently until well blended.

Return to the heat and simmer until the mixture begins to thicken - it should reach the consistency of a creamy soup.

Transfer to individual warmed bowls. Decorate with chopped almonds and serve immediately.

cook's tip

Look for the sweet potatoes with a pinkish skin and yellow flesh, which give a good colour to this dessert.

Dates Stuffed with Spanish Marzipan

15 minutes to the table

method

To make the Spanish marzipan, sift the sugar into a bowl, then stir in the almonds. Sprinkle over the almond extract. Gradually add a little water, ¼ teaspoon at a time, until the mixture comes together and can be pressed into a ball.

Knead the marzipan with your hands and then on a work surface lightly dusted with icing sugar until smooth. It is now ready to be used, or can be wrapped in clingfilm and stored in the refrigerator for up to 3 days.

To stuff the dates, use a small knife to slice along the length of each date, then open out and remove and discard the stone. Break off small pieces of the marzipan, mould each into a 'log' and press into a date. Arrange the dates on a plate and serve with coffee after dinner.

MAKES 12–14

ingredients
12–14 ready-to-eat dried dates

SPANISH MARZIPAN
70 g/2½ oz icing sugar, plus extra
   for dusting
70 g/2½ oz ground almonds
¼ tsp almond extract

Warm Fruit Nests
20 minutes to the table

method

Preheat the oven to 180°C/350°F/Gas Mark 4. Brush 4 small tartlet tins with a little of the oil.

Cut the filo pastry into 16 squares measuring about 12 cm/4½ inches. Brush each square with the remaining oil and use to line the tartlet tins. Use 4 sheets in each tin, and stagger each sheet so that you have a star-shaped effect.

Transfer to a baking sheet and bake in the preheated oven for 7-8 minutes until golden. Transfer to a wire rack to cool slightly.

Meanwhile, put the berries, sugar and mixed spice in a saucepan over a medium heat and heat, stirring gently, until warmed through. Reduce the heat and simmer, stirring, for 10 minutes. Remove from the heat and drain.

Using a slotted spoon, divide the berry mixture between the pastry cases. Decorate with mint sprigs and serve warm with cream.

SERVES 4

ingredients

2-3 tbsp lemon oil

8 sheets filo pastry,
   thawed if frozen

250 g/9 oz fresh blueberries

250 g/9 oz fresh raspberries

250 g/9 oz fresh blackberries

3 tbsp caster sugar

1 tsp ground mixed spice

fresh mint sprigs, to decorate

double cream, to serve

Spiced French Toast with Seasonal Berries

20 minutes to the table

SERVES 4

ingredients

4 eggs, plus 1 egg white
¼ tsp ground cinnamon
¼ tsp ground allspice
4 slices thick white bread
1 tbsp unsalted butter, melted
fresh mint sprigs, to decorate

BERRIES

90 g/3¼ oz caster sugar
4 tbsp freshly squeezed orange juice
300 g/10½ oz mixed fresh seasonal
   berries, such as strawberries,
   raspberries and blueberries, hulled

method

Preheat the oven to 220°C/425°F/Gas Mark 7. Put the eggs and egg white in a large, shallow bowl or dish and whisk together with a fork. Add the cinnamon and allspice and whisk until well combined.

To prepare the berries, put the sugar and orange juice in a saucepan over a low heat, bring to the boil and cook, stirring, until the sugar has dissolved. Add the berries, then remove from the heat and leave to cool for 10 minutes.

Meanwhile, soak the bread slices in the egg mixture for about 1 minute on each side. Brush a large baking sheet with the melted butter and lay the bread slices on the sheet. Bake in the preheated oven for 5–7 minutes, or until lightly browned. Turn the slices over and bake for a further 2–3 minutes.

To serve, cut each slice of toast diagonally in half, put on a serving plate and spoon over the berries. Decorate with mint sprigs.

cook's tip

This oven-baked method of making French Toast uses much less fat than the usual shallow-fried version and makes it easy to produce larger quantities.

Empanadas of Banana and Chocolate

30 minutes to the table

method

Preheat the oven to 190°C/375°F/Gas Mark 5. Peel and dice the bananas, then put in a bowl. Add the caster sugar and lemon juice and stir until well combined. Stir in the chocolate.

Lay 1 long rectangular sheet of filo pastry out on a work surface and brush with butter, keeping the remaining filo covered with a clean, damp tea towel.

Put a couple of teaspoons of the banana and chocolate mixture in one corner of the pastry, then fold over into a triangular shape to enclose the filling. Continue to fold in a triangular shape until the filo is completely wrapped around the filling.

Dust the parcel with icing sugar and cinnamon. Put on a large baking sheet. Repeat the process with the remaining filo and filling.

Bake in the preheated oven for 15 minutes, or until the little pastries are golden. Remove from the oven and serve hot – warn people that the filling will be very hot.

cook's tip

You could use ready-made puff pastry instead of filo for a more puffed-up effect.

MAKES 16

ingredients

2 bananas

1-2 tsp caster sugar

juice of ¼ lemon

175-200 g/6-7 oz plain chocolate, broken into small pieces

about 8 sheets filo pastry, halved lengthways

melted butter or vegetable oil, for brushing

icing sugar, for dusting

ground cinnamon, for dusting

Index

A
apples
Apple Fritters 64
Apple Pancakes with
Maple Syrup Butter 62
Toffee Apple Slices 55

B
Baked Banana with Sin-free
Chocolate Sauce 52
bananas
Baked Banana with Sin-free
Chocolate Sauce 52
Banana Soufflés 82
Chocolate Banana
Sundae 21
Empanadas of Banana
and Chocolate 95
Thai Bananas 38
berries
Berry Sauce 45
Spiced French Toast
with Seasonal Berries 92
bread
Spiced French Toast
with Seasonal Berries 92
Danish Layered Cake 80

C
Caribbean Pineapple 36
Chargrilled Fruit 41
chocolate
Baked Banana with Sin-free
Chocolate Sauce 52
Chocolate Almond Balls 12
Chocolate Banana
Sundae 21
Chocolate Pancakes with
Berry Compôte 16
Chocolate Popcorn 27
Chocolate Sauce 45
Chocolate Squares 18
Chocolate Zabaglione 15
Empanadas of Banana
and Chocolate 95

Mocha Coconut
Clusters 25
Mocha Fondue 10
Snowy Chocolate
Crispies 22
Churros 70
coconut
Mini Coconut Pancakes 67
Mocha Coconut Clusters 25

D
Danish Layered Cake 80
Dates Stuffed with
Spanish Marzipan 89

E
Empanadas of Banana
and Chocolate 95

F
Figs with Orange
Blossom 33
Flambé Peaches 56
French Toast, Spiced with
Seasonal Berries 92
fruit
Apple Fritters 64
Apple Pancakes with
Maple Syrup Butter 62
Baked Banana with Sin-free
Chocolate Sauce 52
Banana Soufflés 82
Caribbean Pineapple 36
Chargrilled Fruit 41
Chocolate Banana
Sundae 21
Empanadas of Banana
and Chocolate 95
Figs with Orange
Blossom 33
Flambé Peaches 56
Lemon Posset 30
Mixed Fruit Salad 46
Pineapple Bake 61
Poached Mixed Spice
Pears 68

Summer Fruit
Nectarines 35
Thai Bananas 38
Tropical Fruit Fool 42
Warm Fruit Compôte 48
Warm Fruit Nests 91

I
ice cream sauces 45

L
lemons
Lemon Posset 30
Syllabub 76
lime
Meringue with Lime Cream
and Raspberries 85

M
Meringue with Lime
Cream and Raspberries 85
Mexican Glazed Pumpkin 59
Mini Coconut Pancakes 67
Mixed Fruit Salad 46
Mocha Coconut Clusters 25
Mocha Fondue 10

N
nectarines
Summer Fruit
Nectarines 35

O
Orange-Blossom Cream 33

P
pancakes
Chocolate Pancakes with
Berry Compôte 16
Mini Coconut Pancakes 67
peaches
Flambé Peaches 56
pears
Poached Mixed Spice
Pears 68
pineapple
Caribbean Pineapple 36

Pineapple Bake 61
Poached Mixed Spice
Pears 68
Popcorn, Chocolate 27
Port Sauce 45
pumpkin
Mexican Glazed
Pumpkin 59

Q
Quick Tiramisù 79

R
raspberries
Meringue with Lime Cream
and Raspberries 85

S
sauces
Berry Sauce 45
Chocolate Sauce 45
Port Sauce 45
Sin-free Chocolate
Sauce 52
Snowy Chocolate Crispies 22
Spiced French Toast with
Seasonal Berries 92
Sponge Cake with
Custard 73
Summer Fruit Nectarines 35
Sweet Potato Dessert 86
Syllabub 76

T
Thai Bananas 38
Tiramisù 79
Toffee Apple Slices 55
Tropical Fruit Fool 42

W
Warm Fruit Compôte 48
Warm Fruit Nests 91

Z
Zabaglione, Chocolate 15